IMAGES
of America

BOSTON'S WEST END

D1212200

Posing in front of the Heath Christian Center in their "Sunday best" are, from left to right, as follows: (front row) Fred Fergar, Jake Cohen, Fred Rudy, and Joe Deliven; (back row) Archie Sorocky, Yano Passanisi, Zip DeLuca, Mike Cataldo, Ralphy Page, and Hubbie Baker. (Courtesy of the West End Historical Association.)

IMAGES
of America

BOSTON'S WEST END

Anthony Mitchell Sammarco

ARCADIA

Published by Arcadia Publishing,
an imprint of Tempus Publishing, Inc.
2 Cumberland Street
Charleston, SC 29401

Printed in Great Britain.

Library of Congress Catalog Card Number: 98-87140

For all general information contact Arcadia Publishing at:
Telephone 843-853-2070
Fax 843-853-0044
E-Mail arcadia@charleston.net

For customer service and orders:
Toll-Free 1-888-313-BOOK

Visit us on the internet at http://www.arcadiaimages.com

Greeting Maurice J. Tobin—mayor of Boston from 1938 to 1944—upon his visit to the West End just after his election is Mrs. Naples (on the right) and John B. Hynes (on the left), who would later serve as mayor of Boston from 1950 to 1959. (Courtesy of the West End Historical Association.)

CONTENTS

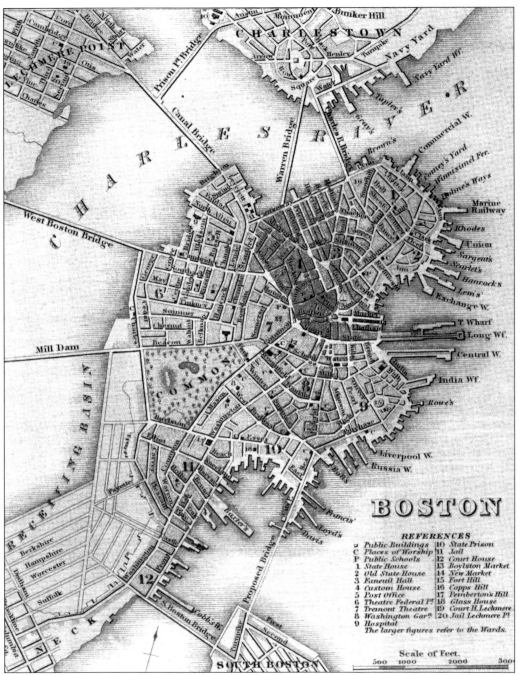

A map of Boston in 1822 shows the 800-acre peninsula that had not materially changed in size since it was settled and named Boston in 1630. Connected to the mainland at Roxbury by a narrow strip of land known as "The Neck," the West End was the upper left-hand side just to the left of the Mill Pond (the present area of North Station).

INTRODUCTION

The West End of Boston exists today only in the memory of Bostonians of middle age or older and in the hearts of the former residents who once lived there—the perennial "West Enders." A once thriving neighborhood that was bound by Beacon Hill, the Charles River, and the present city hall plaza, this unique and special place was obliterated between 1958 and 1960 in the quest of "urban renewal."

Once a place of fashion in the early 19th century, the old West End was the site of Bulfinch-designed mansions of the Boodt, Apthorp, Coolidge, and Otis families. The Harrison Gray Otis House, now the headquarters of the Society for the Preservation of New England Antiquities, still remains at 141 Cambridge Street adjacent to the Old West Church. An elegant neoclassical brick mansion, it stands forlorn along a street that was once a major thoroughfare connecting downtown Boston to the West Boston Bridge, spanning the Charles River. Along this road was once a thriving neighborhood that had accessibility to town, and was often referred to as an elegant oasis with trees and green space bound by the Charles River. Though the West End was no longer a fashionable neighborhood after the mid-19th century, its maze of streets became home to successive waves of immigrant groups and native Americans whose cultures and traditions enhanced the definition of a "West Ender." Without wealth, nor obvious material advantages, the West End community became the epitome of a mixed neighborhood—with African-American, Jewish, Polish, Italian, and Irish residents living and worshipping side by side. According to Chief Justice Elijah Adlow, the West End was "a busy community, seething with the hum of voices and housing a multitude of lately arrived Americans."

However, following World War II, Boston began a project of "urban renewal" that was designed to rid the city of unwanted slums, replacing these areas with modern housing. The areas of Boston's South End and West End were targeted as "slums" and saw large-scale demolition of extant housing stock. During this period of time John B. Hynes, mayor of Boston from 1950 to 1959, instituted a series of development projects throughout the city that, it was hoped, would spur on the dormant economy. Cutting a wide swath through the area of the waterfront, the Central Artery divided the North End, but was to provide convenience for those who once drove through the maze of century-old streets. In the neighborhoods, the "urban renewal" of Boston was partly financed through the Housing Act of 1949; the funding, administered by the Boston Housing Authority, was to finance new housing projects such as

Fidelis Way in Brighton (1950), the Cathedral Project in the South End (1951), Bromley Heath in Roxbury (1954), Franklin Field in Dorchester (1954), and Columbia Point in Dorchester (1954). These new housing projects, primarily built for returning servicemen after WW II, added to the woefully inadequate housing stock, but large tracts of extant housing were demolished in such places as the South End and South Boston. The inevitability of "urban renewal" in the West End seemed certain, looking at the situation in retrospect, but though the area had been referred to as a slum by the city, it was still home to about seven thousand residents.

The devastating destruction of the West End was described by Abbott Lowell Cummings, former director of the Society for the Preservation of New England Antiquities, as "two large-scale land clearance projects in Boston's early West End during 1960 and 1961 [that] have created a devastation here unmatched since that of the fire of 1872 in the downtown area." In actuality, the area was simply swept away with only a few buildings, two churches, and the buildings of the Massachusetts General Hospital surviving to provide a shocking contrast to the once-thriving neighborhood.

By the mid-1960s, under the term of mayor John F. Collins, the West End began to rise again—as in the prophecy of the phoenix arising from the ashes. The old West End was replaced by a new one that consisted of high-rise, luxury apartment buildings with panoramic views of Boston, the Charles River, and Cambridge. The new West End had no room for those who once called this acre of earth home. Charles River Park, composed of high-rise, luxury apartment buildings, was developed to create an urbane and livable space, with underground parking and accessibility to downtown offices. It was a far cry from the once lively, ethnically charged neighborhood that was described by Herbert Gans, the noted sociologist and author of *The Urban Villagers*, as "a good place to live."

One
THE EARLY WEST END

Looking west from Bowdoin Square in 1822, the old West End was a fashionable residential district in the early 19th century. In the center is the Bulfinch-designed duplex of the Blake and Tuckerman families, with the Armstrong and Boodt Houses on the left and the Parkman, Chardon, and Bulfinch Houses on the right. Known as Bowdoin Square in memory of Governor James Bowdoin, it was a charming neighborhood greatly enhanced by the designs of Charles Bulfinch.

The Optimo Cigar Store was housed in an early-19th-century three-story house near the corner of Spring and Poplar Streets. On the left is the Pink Dahlia, a popular West End spa. (Courtesy of the West End Historical Association.)

Members of the volunteer fire department pump a fire engine in front of the home of Thomas Melvill (1751–1832), a departed member of the fire company, on Green Street in 1832. Water would be dumped in the tub of these horse-drawn fire engines and then the levers would be pumped to propel a stream of water at a fire. The Green Street Church, built in 1826, stands next to the Melvill House; it was later the Church of the Advent from 1844 to 1864.

The Bulfinch House was a three-story Colonial mansion facing Bowdoin Square that was built by Dr. Thomas Bulfinch upon his marriage to Judith Colman. This was the birthplace of noted architect Charles Bulfinch in 1763, and ironically the site of his lamented death in 1844.

Charles Bulfinch (1763–1844) was a "gentleman architect" whose sense of style and proportion transformed Boston's built environment into a neoclassical interpretation of the European model. Graduated from Harvard in 1781, Bulfinch's grand tour of Europe not only awakened his architectural curiosity, but changed Boston's architectural mask forever.

Harrison Gray Otis (1765–1848) commissioned Charles Bulfinch in 1796 to build a brick, three-story Federal mansion at the corner of Cambridge and Lynde Streets. Adjacent to the Old West Church, the Otis House was an elegant and symmetrical mansion that was the prototype for future Boston houses. Although Otis only lived here for four years, the house survived a plethora of commercial adaptations until it was purchased in 1916 by the Society for the Preservation of New England Antiquities.

Joseph Coolidge (1747–1829) lived in a three-story Federal mansion that was designed by Charles Bulfinch in 1792 and built facing Bowdoin Square between Temple and Bowdoin Streets. With its Ionic pilasters supporting a cornice surmounted by an urn-embellished roof balustrade, it was a truly "noble mansion," as Bulfinch described it upon its demolition in 1843.

The Joseph Coolidge Jr. House was designed by Charles Bulfinch, and shared many of the neoclassical details of the father's house. Coolidge was married to Elizabeth Bulfinch, the architect's sister, and it is safe to assume that Bulfinch lavished additional attention on the design of the couple's house in the West End.

The Blake-Tuckerman House was a duplex built in 1815 for Samuel Parkman. Designed by Charles Bulfinch and built of Chelmsford granite, the house faced Bowdoin Square between Cambridge and Green Streets. Parkman was the proprietor of the brick market at the corner of Cambridge and Grove Streets, which Bulfinch designed and built in 1810 for West End residents.

The Kirk Boodt House was designed by Bulfinch and built on the corner of Cambridge and Bulfinch Streets (now the site of the Saltonstall Building) in 1804. An elegant, three-story neoclassical mansion, it would eventually be remodeled as the Revere House, a well-known hotel in 19th-century Boston.

Kirk Boodt was agent of the Locks and Canal Company in Lowell and an investor in the mills built at Lowell, Massachusetts. The Boodt Mill on the Merrimac River provided a great fortune for the investors. Known as the "captain of industry" in Lowell, Boodt was also well respected in Boston.

SEA WATER BATHS.

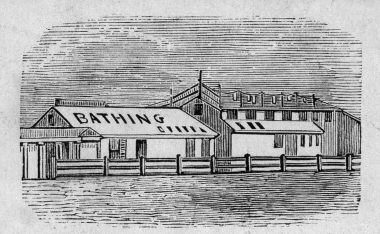

The Public are respectfully informed that the

CRAGIE BRIDGE
BATHING ESTABLISHMENT,

Foot of Leverett Street,

Is in complete order, and that WARM, COLD, SHOWER and

SWIMMING BATHS

Can be had Daily, from 5 A. M. to 10 P. M.   An excellent
Salt Water Soap is furnished bathers.

☞ SEPARATE APARTMENTS FOR LADIES, ☜

Single Tickets 12 1-2 Cents—or 10 for $1.

Season Tickets for the Swimming-Bath.

BOSTON, JULY 1, 1851.   **C. BRUCE.**

Sea-water baths were available for 12 1/2¢ (or, for true frugal Yankees, at ten baths for $1) in a
large building at the foot of Leverett Street in the West End. Built at the entrance to the
Craigie Bridge, which spanned the Charles River and connected the West End to Cambridge,
this bathing house was well equipped with "warm, cold, shower and swimming baths."
(Courtesy of the Paine Collection.)

The Almshouse was designed by Charles Bulfinch and built in 1801 on Leverett Street in the old West End. An impressive building with a central pavilion with flanking wings, it replaced the old Poor House that had been on Park Street. Designed as a brick structure 276 feet in length "with white marble fascias, imposts, and keystones, it had four staircases ten feet wide and a central hall forty by fifty feet."

Samuel Stillman Pierce (1807–1881) was the proprietor of S.S. Pierce & Company, Boston's leading 19th-century specialty and gourmet food store. He opened his business in 1831 at the corner of Tremont and Court Streets and lived in the West End until he moved to the newly fashionable South End in 1851.

Pemberton Square was a fashionable, residential square just off Bowdoin Square. Brick townhouses of uniform height were ranged around a central green space planted with trees, attracting members of the Sigorney, Winthrop, Bowditch, Lowell, Brooks, and Shattuck families before the area was swept away and the Suffolk County Court House was built here just before the turn of the century.

Numbers 16 to 26 Staniford Street, looking north toward Green Street, illustrate the beauty of the West End in the 1880s. These small houses, especially the mansard-roofed house in the center, were charming residences near to downtown but far enough away to allow for pleasant, stylish living in the mid-19th century. (Courtesy of David Rooney.)

Howard Street, originally known as Southack's Court until 1821, was once a residential street that had elegant houses designed by Charles Bulfinch, such as the Stephen Codman House on the right. In the 20th century, Howard Street was well-known for the Old Howard, a vaudeville and later burlesque house that most men in town visited at one time or another.

Brigham's Market was the quintessential market in Boston at the turn of the century. Here a straw-boatered clerk takes an order from a young girl as slabs of meat await the cleaver, or the attention of the cat who is asleep under the butcher block! (Courtesy of the West End Historical Association.)

The National Horse and Carriage Mart on Portland Street was "since 1875 . . . the center of auction sales of horses, carriages, etc." Notice the huge head of a horse painted on the side wall of the mart as an advertisement that could be seen from blocks away.

The Charles Street Jail was designed by Gridley J. Fox Bryant and built in 1851 of rough-hewn granite at the corner of Cambridge and Charles Streets. The jail originally had 220 cells, each 8 by 11 feet, with thick walls of granite. The structure replaced an earlier jail (the old Almshouse) on Leverett Street in the West End.

A paddy wagon, often referred to as a "Black Maria," was a horse-drawn conveyance that brought prisoners to and from the Charles Street Jail in the mid-19th century. A prisoner is helped into the wagon as two men on the right observe a signboard that reads "Road to Ruin."

The members of the Boston Police Department assigned to Police Station No. 3 pose for a group portrait about 1895 in front of police headquarters. (Courtesy of the West End Historical Association.)

A police chief and his driver stop in front of Police Station No. 1 in their Buick police car about 1905. To the left of the policeman standing against the car is the entrance to the Central Fire Station. Notice the hand-operated bell mounted to the hood of the police car—a swift pull to the rope sounded their approach! (Courtesy of the West End Historical Association.)

The Revere House was an elegant hotel and an 1847 enlargement of the old Kirk Boodt House in Bowdoin Square. Designed by William Washburn, the hotel was "a famous resort for over three-quarters of a century, and has entertained some of the most eminent men and women" of the 19th century. The famous hotel was demolished in 1919 and a fire station was built on its site, which was eventually replaced by a state office building.

The Central Hotel was a small, inexpensive, residential hotel on Green Street that rented rooms and small parlor-suites. (Courtesy of David Rooney.)

Martin Lomasney (1860–1933), known as the "Boston Mahatma," was ward boss of the West End for over three decades. A political force to be reckoned with, Lomasney was eulogized by the Hendricks Club, which he led during his lifetime. The club stated its mission after his death as follows: "It is our duty to carry on our late leader's splendid traditions through the coming years. That we remain loyal to our community and to one another would have been his fondest wish. We can do no less."

The Hancock Building was at the corner of Cambridge and Grove Streets. The Hendricks Club occupied the top floor for many years. (Courtesy of the West End Historical Association.)

This snow remover was used on city streets in the early 1950s to remove snow on a conveyor belt. Once filled, the truck would dump the accumulated snow into Boston Harbor. (Courtesy of the West End Historical Association.)

The Boston Smoker Cigar Factory was at the corner of Cambridge and Chambers Streets. Photographed in 1911, the former residence also housed Balkan's Tailor shop, the Atlas Hand Laundry, and a painting and glazing shop. (Courtesy of David Rooney.)

Bowdoin Square, seen looking west in 1934, was a bustling intersection that had Bowdoin Theatre on the right and stores on all sides. The Bowdoin Square Garage can be seen on the left corner. (Courtesy of the West End Historical Association.)

The former Harrison Gray Otis House had storefronts built in front of it by the turn of the century, with a Chinese laundry and haberdashery shop marring the elegance of Bulfinch's design. Cambridge Street would eventually be widened and the Otis House moved back. The Old West Church can be seen on the far right. (Courtesy of David Rooney.)

Cambridge Street was lined with bars, shops, and rooms to let by the "day or week," and led to Bowdoin Square. The cupola of the Old West Church can be seen on the left. (Courtesy of the West End Historical Association.)

Looking from the corner of Cambridge and Lynde Streets, the former Old West Church—used as a branch library at this time—can be seen on the left. Mid-19th-century townhouses are on the far right at the corner of Staniford Street. (Courtesy of David Rooney.)

Two
HOSPITALS OF THE WEST END

Looking east toward the Massachusetts General Hospital from the Charles River in 1853, the Bulfinch-designed hospital can be seen on the left and the Harvard Medical School on the right. Notice the pilings that were driven into the flats that were later filled and extended for Charles Street and Storrow Drive. (Courtesy of the Massachusetts General Hospital.)

The Massachusetts General Hospital was founded in 1799 and incorporated in 1811. An imposing granite hospital, it was designed by Charles Bulfinch in 1817 and built on Fruit Street near the West Boston (now Longfellow) Bridge. On the far left can be seen the Harvard Medical School and in the distance is the Mc Lean Asylum in Somerville. Named for John McLean, whose bequest was to benefit both the hospital and asylum, it moved to Waverly in Belmont in 1895.

Bulfinch's design for the Massachusetts General Hospital incorporated a colonnade of granite columns that supported a pediment, with flanking staircases. The design was probably inspired by the Villa Foscati; it is a Palladio design that creates as timeless a sense of classicism as do those of Bulfinch.

William Thomas Green Morton (1819–1868) was painted by W. Hudson Jr. in 1845. Known as the "revealer of painless surgery," his discovery caused him great bitterness when others claimed the honor. Today, the Ether Monument in the Boston Public Garden honors Morton, but his monument at Mount Auburn Cemetery reads as follows: "Inventor and revealer of anesthetic inhalation Before whom, in all time, surgery was agony By whom pain in surgery was averted and annulled Since whom science has control of pain."

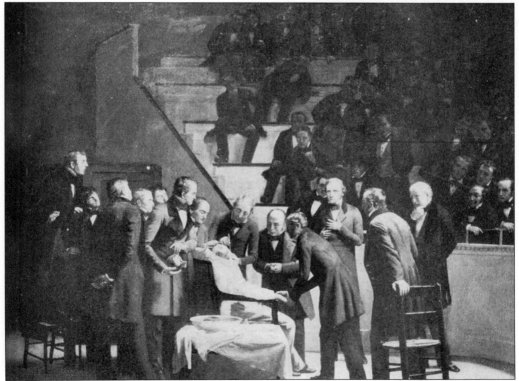

In this painting, artist Robert Hinckley depicts the first operation with ether at the Massachusetts General Hospital on October 16, 1846. Dr. John Collins Warren (1778–1856) performed surgery on Gilbert Abbott in the Ether Dome of the hospital.

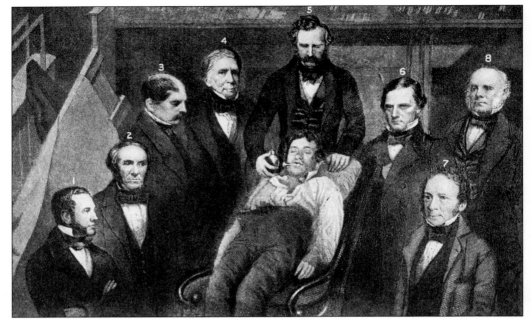

Dr. J. Collins Warren stands on the left of Gilbert Abbott, who has been prepped for the removal of a tumor on the jaw. Drs. Henry Bigelow (1), Augustus Gould (2), J. Warren Mason (3), J. Collins Warren (4), William Morton (5), Samuel Parkman (6), George Hayward (7), and T.D. Townsend (8) witnessed what Dr. Weir Mitchell called the "Death of Pain" when ether was used to dull Abbott's senses. Dr. J. Collins Warren remarked that the technique "is no humbug."

The granite wings flanking Bulfinch's original design were enlarged in the late 19th century, following the same lines and use of Chelmsford granite. From the time the hospital was founded with Drs. Warren, Jackson, Gorham, Jacob Bigelow, and Channing in 1811, it has grown to become one of the leading hospitals in the world.

Looking west, the Charles River lies just beyond the grounds of the Massachusetts General Hospital. The well-manicured lawns and pathways in front of the Bulfinch building give a distinctly Victorian feeling to this photograph. (Courtesy of the West End Historical Association.)

Chimneys project from the roofs of the hospitals in the foreground. The dome of the Massachusetts General Hospital can be seen on the left and the dome of the Massachusetts State House, also by Charles Bulfinch and completed in 1798, can be seen on the right. (Courtesy of the West End Historical Association.)

A group of nurses and training nurses poses for a formal portrait at the turn of the century. White caps denoted registered nurses, while black-banded caps denoted student nurses. (Courtesy of the Massachusetts General Hospital.)

In 1898, during the Spanish-American War, Boston's hospitals erected tents on their grounds to offer shelter to the large number of soldiers returning home with typhoid fever or malaria. It was thought that fresh air would be beneficial to their recovery. The head nurse is Hannah Churchill and four of her student nurses (with black bands on their caps) surround her. (Courtesy of the Massachusetts General Hospital.)

Ward A (also known as the Warren Ward in honor of Dr. J. Collins Warren) was built in 1873. The center chimney had fireplaces on all four sides providing warmth for the patients, whose beds lined the exterior walls upon the plan of an army field hospital. (Courtesy of the Massachusetts General Hospital.)

A horse-drawn ambulance was the means of conveyance for patients arriving at the Massachusetts General Hospital in the late 19th century. Earlier in the 19th century, patients were often brought to the hospital by boat, as the flats along the Charles allowed for smooth transport. (Courtesy of the Massachusetts General Hospital.)

The superintendent's house at the Massachusetts General Hospital was a small brick structure at the corner of Allen and Blossom Streets. This house was moved in 1980 to the corner of Cambridge and Blossom Streets, and restored by the hospital after preservationists urged its saving. (Courtesy of David Rooney.)

The rotunda of the Moseley Memorial Building was a dramatic space that has since been remodeled. Portraits of those associated with the hospital adorn piers while a flag, on the left, honors the number of hospital associates then serving in WW II. (Courtesy of the Massachusetts General Hospital.)

The Proctor Building was erected in 1903 as the Outpatient Department. (Courtesy of the Massachusetts General Hospital.)

A view of the West End from the Suffolk County Court House just prior to WW II shows a densely built-up neighborhood of Boston. Cambridge Street can be seen in the foreground with the Harrison Gray Otis House and the Old West Church on the far right. Other than the Charles Street Jail and the various buildings of the Massachusetts General Hospital, the neighborhood ceased to exist as a place of residence after "urban renewal" was instituted. (Courtesy of the Massachusetts General Hospital.)

On opening day at the George Robert White Building, doctors, nurses, and dignitaries look on as the ribbon is being cut. The building was named for philanthropist George Robert White, whose fund still supports the health services throughout Boston. (Courtesy of the West End Historical Association.)

The construction of the White Building would greatly expand the campus of the Massachusetts General Hospital. By the late 1950s, the buildings included the Bulfinch (1821), Thayer (1883), Eye and Ear Infirmary (1898), Walcott House (1913), Moseley (1916), Phillips House (1917), Baker (1930), White (1939), Vincent Burnham (1947), Research (1950), Bartlett Hall (1952), and Warren (1956). (Courtesy of the West End Historical Association.)

Harvard Medical School was founded in 1782 through the efforts of Dr. John Warren. Moving from Cambridge to Boston in 1810, it was to "secure those advantages for clinical instruction and for the practical anatomy which are found only in large cities." This school was built in 1846 on North Grove Street and here it remained until it moved to the Back Bay later in the century, after which it was used as the Harvard Dental School.

The Massachusetts Charitable Eye and Ear Infirmary was founded in 1824 by Drs. Edward Reynolds and John Jeffries. The infirmary grew to such proportions that a new building was erected in 1850 at the corner of Charles and Cambridge Streets.

The Boston Lying In Hospital was located in the West End until it moved to the Fenway of Boston in the early 20th century. Here, the hospital has been secured prior to its demolition. (Courtesy of David Rooney.)

Mount Sinai Hospital was located at 130 Chambers Street, where it offered outpatient medical care for the rapidly expanding Jewish community of Boston. Eventually, this five-room hospital expanded and became Beth Israel Hospital. (Courtesy of the West End Historical Association.)

Three
PLACES OF WORSHIP

An altar boy carries a crucifix high above those participating in a May Procession from Saint Joseph's Church in the late 1940s. Parishes in the Archdiocese of Boston would hold processions through the streets of the parish during the month of May with children who had received their first holy communion and members of the Sunday school participating. (Courtesy of the West End Historical Association.)

The Brattle Square Church was built in 1772 on Brattle Street near Bowdoin Square. A commodious church designed by Thomas Dawes, it was a place of worship for a century until a new church, designed by H.H. Richardson, was built at the corner of Commonwealth Avenue and Clarendon Street in the Back Bay.

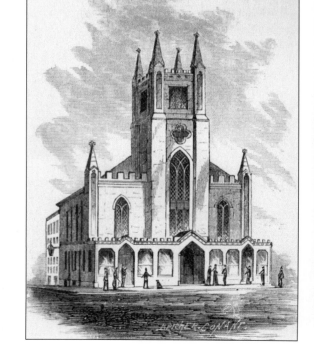

The Bowdoin Square Baptist Church once stood on Bowdoin Square at the present site of the telephone building. Built in 1840 of un-hammered granite, its tower was 110 feet high.

The Old West Church was designed by Asher Benjamin (1773–1845) and built in 1806 at the corner of Cambridge and Lynde Streets, replacing an earlier 1737 church razed in 1775 by the British. A once fashionable church, the West End had affected its congregation to the point that the last service was held in 1892. From 1896 to 1940, the building was used as the West End Branch of the Boston Public Library. Since 1964, a Methodist congregation has worshipped here.

The interior of the Old West Church, looking toward the organ from the pulpit, had an elegant interior with box pews and a gallery clock by Simon Willard of Roxbury. The pulpit was removed in 1895 when the church was remodeled as the West End Branch of the Boston Public Library and installed at the First Parish Church in Dorchester. The superb Fisk tracker-action pipe organ survives to sound forth at frequent organ concerts.

The Heath Christian Center was founded by the Baptist Church in Bowdoin Square as a settlement house at 38 Chambers Street. As a mission of the Baptist Church, it evolved as a social center for residents of the West End. (Courtesy of the West End Historical Association.)

The North Russell Street Synagogue was one of six temples in the West End in the early 20th century. Though some were small places of worship, the North Russell Street Synagogue had a large congregation. (Courtesy of the West End Historical Association.)

The Chassidic congregation of Grand Rabbi Pinchas D. Horowitz was founded just before World War I in the West End. The congregation worshipped in this brick duplex house at 87 Poplar Street at the corner of Brighton Street until the early 1940s, when it moved to Dorchester. (Courtesy of the West End Historical Association.)

The facade of Anshe Vilna of Boston was a highly patterned brick design on Phillips Street on the western slope of Beacon Hill. Built in 1919 for a Lithuanian congregation that was founded at the turn of the century, this was one of a half dozen temples in the West End. (Courtesy of the West End Historical Association.)

Saint Joseph's Church was designed by Alexander Parris and was originally built for the Twelfth Congregation Church (Unitarian). Here in a photograph just before WW II, the church was encircled by a cast-iron fence and was witness to never-ending street life. Bernie Corcoran, Mario Manzelli, and Nina Bottari stop to chat at the corner of McLean Street. (Courtesy of the West End Historical Association.)

The sanctuary of Saint Joseph's Church was remodeled after Vatican II, with an elegant entablature enframing a late-19th-century painting of *The Crucifixion*. The figure of The Holy Spirit descends from the broken arch pediment, as a form of inspiration and guidance through Jesus Christ. (Courtesy of Saint Joseph's Church.)

The altar of Our Lady of Ostrobrama (Saint Mary's) Church in the West End was a simple design with angels and statues of saints surrounding it. (Courtesy of the West End Historical Association.)

The main altar of Our Lady of Ostrobrama (Saint Mary's) Church had statues of Saint Joseph and Saint Theresa on either side. An image of the Virgin Mary, for whom the church was named, is high above the altar. (Courtesy of the West End Historical Association.)

Children who had recently made their first holy communion participate in a May Procession in the West End in the early 1950s. (Courtesy of the West End Historical Association.)

Father Powers participates in a May Procession on McLean Street in 1940. Father Powers was a popular priest at Saint Joseph's Church, and was well known throughout the West End by residents of all faiths. (Courtesy of the West End Historical Association.)

Participating in a May Procession in 1950 are Lou Ferullo and Walter Downs. Though a Marian feast, the May Procession often featured a statue of Saint Joseph, the husband of the Virgin Mary. (Courtesy of the West End Historical Association.)

Bearing a statue of the Blessed Virgin Mary in a May Procession are Joe Zanelli and Billy Landolfi in the front. (Courtesy of the West End Historical Association.)

Carolyn Addessa as a May queen leads young children in a Saint Joseph's Church May Procession in the mid-1950s. Young men bear a statue of the Infant of Prague in the rear. (Courtesy of the West End Historical Association.)

The Saint Joseph's Church May Procession of 1954 enters Mc Lean Street with young children bearing signs with religious verses. (Courtesy of the West End Historical Association.)

During one of the May Processions in the 1940s in the West End, Father Regan stops to speak with Marie Capachiette, Nina Bottari, and ? Gianino. (Courtesy of the West End Historical Association.)

Ensuring that the children in this May Procession march in formation and behave themselves is a nun in a traditional habit. (Courtesy of the West End Historical Association.)

Gathering in front of an electrified shrine that holds the statue of Saint Domenic is a crowd of faithful. These parishioners often pinned paper money to cascading ribbons to honor the saint and to allow the society to fund good works during the ensuing year. (Courtesy of the West End Historical Association.)

Some of the officers of the Society of Saint Domenic stand before a banner carried in a street possession. Each member of the society wore a white ribbon around her neck with a medal of Saint Domenic. (Courtesy of the West End Historical Association.)

A young boy wears his first-communion suit as he stands on a flight of makeshift stairs at the Feast of Saint Domenic. Children who had recently received their first holy communion would often wear their white suit or dress for weeks after the event! (Courtesy of the West End Historical Association.)

Not all feast attendees were there to follow the procession of the saint through the streets of the West End. The youngest of the feasters often rode this carousel, which would be driven by Domenic Salamone from feast to feast, thrilling every child in the process. (Courtesy of the West End Historical Association.)

The Feast of Saint Domenic was celebrated in 1954 with a procession through the West End. Here, the procession is seen on Hale Street. (Courtesy of the West End Historical Association.)

The Feast of Saint Domenic winds its way down Hale Street, past apartment buildings whose windows are filled to overflowing with residents watching the procession from their windows. (Courtesy of the West End Historical Association.)

A statue of Saint Anthony is bedecked with ribbons, to which have been pinned donations from the devout. (Courtesy of the West End Historical Association.)

Bearing poles that support an icon of the Virgin Mary and the Infant Jesus are men who are partly shrouded by a rich tapestry surrounding the holy image. Donations have been pinned on ribbons falling from the tapestry. (Courtesy of the West End Historical Association.)

The devout often accompanied a saint's statue as it was processed through the streets. Here an elderly woman recites the Rosary as she keeps in step with those accompanying the statue of Saint Domenic. Often, the devout walked barefoot for a special intercession by the saint. (Courtesy of the West End Historical Association.)

A statue of Saint Joseph and the Infant Jesus is paraded through the streets of the West End in the early 1950s. (Courtesy of the West End Historical Association.)

What else would one expect for street food at the feasts but zeppoles? These lightly fried pieces of sweet dough would be dusted with confectioner's sugar before being greedily devoured. (Courtesy of the West End Historical Association.)

By the end of the feast, the annual event of climbing the greased pole brought out agile young men who tried, often in vain, to reach the top of a pole that had been liberally smeared with grease. Their efforts elicited hoots and jeers from the crowd. (Courtesy of the West End Historical Association.)

Four

SCHOOLS

Posing in front of the Wells School in dresses they made themselves are girls who learned to sew through the generosity of Mary Porter Tileston Hemenway. A member of the Boston School Committee, Mrs. Hemenway introduced both sewing and domestic science courses into the curriculum for students who were not matriculating to college. Upon graduation, these girls could sew for themselves or use their skills to earn a living to help support their family before their marriage.

The Wells School was designed by Richards and Park and was built in 1868, serving three generations of West End schoolchildren. An annex was built to accommodate the large student body in 1914, but both school and annex were eventually closed in 1947. (Courtesy of David Rooney.)

The Wendell Phillips School was designed by Nathaniel J. Bradlee and was built in 1861, being named after the great abolitionist and publisher of *The Guardian*. Located at the corner of Phillips and Anderson Streets, it closed in 1940 when it was sold and converted to a technical school. In 1977, the former school was sold for conversion to housing. (Courtesy of David Rooney.)

The Winchell School was designed by Arthur H. Vinal and was built in 1885 at the corner of Blossom and Parkman Streets; after a dramatic increase in the student body, a third floor was added in 1907. During the addition's construction, electric clocks by the Self-Winding Clock Company were installed. The Winchell School closed in 1960. (Courtesy of David Rooney.)

The Mayhew School was built in 1897 at the corner of Chambers and Poplar Streets. Designed by John Lyman Faxon, the school had a double-arched entrance at the corner and fanciful roof dormers. The Mayhew School closed in 1959. (Courtesy of David Rooney.)

The Peter Faneuil School was built in 1910 and named in memory of the great public benefactor who donated Faneuil Hall to the town of Boston in 1742. Designed by Kelley and Graves on Joy Street, it was closed in 1975 and was later used by "Another Course to College," an alternative school, prior to its conversion to apartments in 1994. (Courtesy of David Rooney.)

The William Blackstone School was built in 1916 and named in memory of the Rev. William Blackstone, the first European resident of Beacon Hill. Designed by Harrison H. Atwood and built on Blossom Street, the school was closed in 1959 and eventually demolished in 1977. (Courtesy of David Rooney.)

The basketball team of the William Blackstone School in 1953 included, from left to right, the following: (front row) Sal Palmisano, Jim Spina, Ken Mac Cauley, Richard Worob, Ralph Santosuosso, and Louis Florence; (back row) George Dick, Yanno Viola, Pat Vidette, Richard Rita, and Tony Longo. (Courtesy of the West End Historical Association.)

Standing in front of the impressive cast-iron fence enclosing the Blackstone schoolyard are, from the left, Lillian Worob, Marie Treska, Roseanne Orlando, and Pauline Spinale. (Courtesy of the West End Historical Association.)

Ernest Di Mattia (on the far left) and his shop students pose during class at the William Blackstone School. Two slogans—"Without Tools Man Is Nothing" and "With Tools He Is All"—grace either side of the bulletin board. One can imagine highly glossed spice holders, napkin holders, and cutting boards made by generations of public-school boys. (Courtesy of the West End Historical Association.)

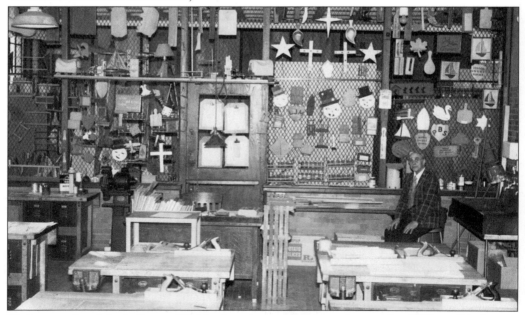

Sitting on the right is Ernest Di Mattia, who taught shop class at the William Blackstone School. Attached to the grill separating the shop from protective storage is a plethora of class projects made by students that includes crosses, snowman heads, and spice racks. Happy were the parents who received these handicrafts after weeks of hard work!

Five

THE CHARLESBANK

A group of children poses for their photograph on the Charlesbank at the turn of the century. Laid out as a green space with grass, trees, and playgrounds on a narrow strip of land between Cambridge and Leverett Streets, it attracted many residents of the area. On the right is the edge of the Charles River, now Storrow Drive.

The Union Boat Club was founded in 1851, and the original clubhouse was a Swiss-style building with piazzas built in 1870 overlooking the Charles River Basin. Having the distinction of introducing on the Charles River the style of rowing without a coxswain, the Union Boat Club has been a popular club in the city since its founding.

The Shingle-style pavilion of the Charles River Embankment was built on the flats of the Charles River, now Storrow Drive. A young lady peers over the metal balustrade that surmounted the granite embankment walls that protected the coastline. The cupola of the Charles Street Jail can be seen rising above the roof.

The Charlesbank Gymnasium was an outdoor playground for children; its rules enforced the segregation of youngsters by sex. The boys had their gymnasium near the West Boston (now Longfellow) Bridge on Cambridge Street, and the girls had theirs near the Craigie Bridge opposite Chambers Street.

Irving Ganek (on the left) and Marvin Black stand in front of an open, canvas-awninged boat at the boat-loading dock at the Esplanade in 1940. For a dime, or a nickel for children, one could enjoy a boat ride around the Charles River Basin. (Courtesy of the West End Historical Association.)

These children tend a Victory Garden that was established on the Charlesbank during WW II. The idea of growing produce on land in the city had been introduced during WW I, and here the young farmers till the soil near Leverett Circle. On the far left can be seen the registry of motor vehicles on Nashua Street. (Courtesy of the West End Historical Association.)

Practice makes perfect, and these children tilled the soil, smoothed it with rakes, and planted seeds for their very own garden. The Elizabeth Peabody House can be seen on the left and apartment buildings on Charles Street are on the right. (Courtesy of the West End Historical Association.)

A portion of the Charlesbank was used as a site for the Hatch Shell, a gift to the city of Boston by Miss Maria Hatch in 1926 in memory of her brother, Edward Hatch. Designed by Richard Shaw and built in 1940 of concrete and granite in an Art Deco-style, seven-layer shell, it has hosted open-air concerts for over five decades. On the far right is Storrow Drive, named in memory of James Jackson Storrow. (Courtesy of the West End Historical Association.)

A group of friends poses in front of the Art-Deco Hatch Shell in the late 1940s; from the top are Pat Hoar, Lena Phillips and Pat, Jackie Hoar, Alice Polonka, and Peggy. Strangely, Pat and Peggy weren't West Enders, so their surnames were not recorded! (Courtesy of the West End Historical Association.)

Abe Greenstein and Lucie Hall mug for the camera in 1944 as they relax on Charles River Beach, a portion of the Charlesbank that is now part of the Esplanade. On the right is the Charles Street Jail and to its left are the buildings of the Massachusetts General Hospital. (Courtesy of the West End Historical Association.)

A young boy fishes on the wrong side of the Charlesbank in the 1950s. The Science Museum (formerly the Museum of Natural History in the Back Bay) on the Charles River Dam can be seen on the left. (Courtesy of the West End Historical Association.)

Sailboats line the dock outside the Joseph Lee Community Boathouse on the Charles River. (Courtesy of the West End Historical Association.)

Joseph Lee was a noted community activist and an advocate of open space and parks for the enjoyment of the public. A resident of South Russell Street, he was a member of the Boston School Committee, as was his father. The elder Lee was often referred to as "the father of the American playground." (Courtesy of the West End Historical Association.)

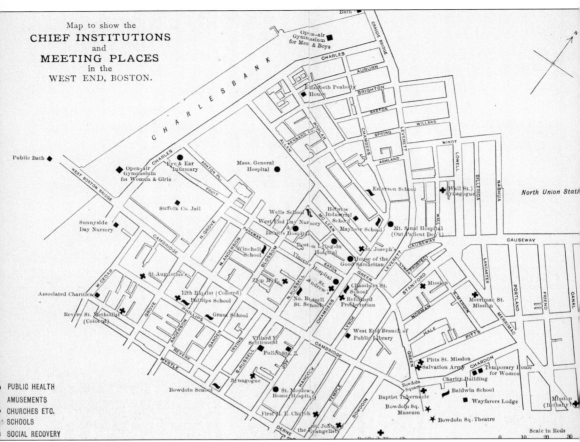

This map shows the chief institutions and meeting places of the West End, a thriving neighborhood in the early 20th century. With schools, hospitals, churches, and such places as the Charlesbank, the Elizabeth Peabody House, the Villard Y, and the Hebrew Industrial School, it was a place where people from all walks of life lived and worked. (Courtesy of the West End Historical Association.)

Six

THE WEST END HOUSE AND ELIZABETH PEABODY HOUSE

Members of the 1955–56 West End House basketball team were, from left to right, as follows: (front row) Jim Guskiewicz, Sal Bellistri, Dom Sarcia, Charlie La Rosa, Roger Jackman, and Joe Russo; (back row) Coach Paul Skiffington, Sam Bottari, Tony Comperchio, Tony Louolo, Pat Videtti, and Director Jack Burnes. (Courtesy of the West End Historical Association.)

The Elizabeth Peabody House was established in 1896 at 156 Chambers Street in the West End, moving to 357 Charles Street in 1912. It was named in memory of Elizabeth Palmer Peabody, whose dedication to the care of children led to the first kindergarten in Boston. The seven-story building, built in 1912, housed a dance hall, gymnasium, library, kitchen, and theater. (Courtesy of David Rooney.)

Unveiling an Elizabeth Peabody House Honor Roll of soldiers and sailors serving in WW II are Mrs. Josephine Roche (on the left) and Mrs. Francis Mc Grath. Unveiled on Veterans Day in 1943, the honor roll included 495 names, including those of five who gave the supreme sacrifice in the defense of their country. (Courtesy of the West End Historical Association.)

Janet Robbins, a social worker at the Elizabeth Peabody House in 1948, offers cookies to children who were in her class. The cookies were served with milk, as it was the Peabody House that in 1902 opened the first pasteurized milk stations in this country. (Courtesy of the West End Historical Association.)

Hazel Hardlaker reads to children at the Elizabeth Peabody House in 1946. On the far right is Patricia Shaw, an observer, who was training in social work. (Courtesy of the West End Historical Association.)

Amateur theatricals were often presented at the Elizabeth Peabody House to raise funds for ongoing activities that benefited the residents of the West End. *The Chimes of Normandy* was presented in 1939 at the Peabody Playhouse, a theater within the Peabody House. (Courtesy of the West End Historical Association.)

Another popular production at the Peabody Playhouse was *The Mikado*. With lavish costumes and stage sets, these theatricals seemed to bring out the whole of the West End. (Courtesy of the West End Historical Association.)

The West End House was built on Blossom Street through the generosity of the George Robert White Fund. (Courtesy of the West End Historical Association.)

James Jackson Storrow (1864–1926) and Helen Osborne Storrow (1864–1944) were influential in the founding of the West End House.

Members of the 1941 Armstrong Juniors basketball team of the West End House were, from left to right, as follows: (front row) Paul Nichols, Nicky Bova, Jimmy Maggio, Assistant Coach Pat Falino, Johnny Nichols, Antonio Almeida, Harold Weinstein, and Nick Albondi; (back row) Johnny Razo, unknown, Peter Nasti, Coach Lonnie Priscio, Johnny Clifford, Joe Gemmato, and Frankie Gulla. (Courtesy of the West End Historical Association.)

The track team of the West End House involved boys of all ages. Seated in the center is Coach Harry Slade, with managers Teddy Red on the left and Henry Seigle on the right. (Courtesy of the West End Historical Association.)

Members of the Storrow Juniors Club of the West End House in 1948 were, from left to right, as follows: (front row) George Berger, Joe Paris, Joe Jackman, Roger Jackman, Dom Strazzula, and Joe Corso; (back row) Bob Nicolosi, Jim Jackman, Sam Pirri, Tom Jackman, Lou Ferrulo, Coach Frank Marinella, Jay Backus, Frank Merowski, Chris Naoum, and Bill Stavre. (Courtesy of the West End Historical Association.)

The 1957 "Romans" basketball team posed for a group photograph. From left to right they are as follows: (front row) Pat Palmisano, Richie Morello, Bobby Morello, Sal Auditore, and Gus Dettore; (back row) Coach Paul "Moose" Camuso, Bob Reid, Tim Creedon, Joe Gallo, Mike Corrente, Tom Bialecki, Ken Smith, and Eddie Real (the basketball referee and Peabody House administrator). The "Romans" were in a league along with the "Junior Dukes," the "Cougars," and the "Olympics." (Courtesy of Richard J. Morello.)

Rooting on Tommy Greb (Consolo) at the West End House are, from left to right, as follows: (front row) Joe Tenullo, Bob Nicolosi, Ed Langone, John Consolo, and Lester Freeman; (back row) Peter Efenchuch, unknown, Guy Consolo, James Mead, and Al Lanza. (Courtesy of the West End Historical Association.)

Members of the West End House "Midgets" basketball team in 1949 were, from left to right, as follows: (front row) Lou Dimuzio, Joe Dolci, Mike De Rosa, Roger Jackman, Dom Strazzula, Joe Corso, and Bill Stavre; (back row) Director Moe Isaacson, Jim Jackman, Tom Jackman, Ron Guarino, and Coach Frank Marinella. (Courtesy of the West End Historical Association.)

The 1956 West End House Varsity lined up for a group portrait. From the left are Joey Cancelleri (the team mascot), Paul Skiffington, L. Glynn, John Marinella, Dom De Fazio, Roger Jackman, Tony Louolo, Joe Russo, Charlie La Rosa, Tom Jackman, Ralph Santosuosso, Bob Mc Menimen, and Eldridge Moore. The inset photograph is of Coach Frank Marinella. (Courtesy of the West End Historical Association.)

Posing after a basketball game in 1941 are, from left to right, as follows: (front row) Walter T., Teddy D., and unknown; (back row) Jackie Block, Saul B., and Teddy ?. (Courtesy of the West End Historical Association.)

Playing in the gym at the West End House is a group of young boys. (Courtesy of the West End Historical Association.)

Martha Mixer reads with young girls at the West End House in the late 1940s. (Courtesy of the West End Historical Association.)

Perched precariously on the jungle gym in the basement of the West End House are a group of young boys. Within a few years a multitude of clubs would entertain these boys after school. (Courtesy of the West End Historical Association.)

Jack Burns, standing on the right, leads boys at the West End House in a song as they are accompanied by a young pianist. Above the upright piano are photographs of various young men who were associated with the West End House just a few decades before. (Courtesy of the West End Historical Association.)

Participating in a game of ping-pong at the West End House is Benjamin Ptaszynski. (Courtesy of the West End Historical Association.)

Intently watching a shot in the pool room of the West End House in 1941 are, from left to right, Robert Kalogeros, Edwin Kaufman, Salvatore Gulla, and Joseph Maccarone. (Courtesy of the West End Historical Association.)

Like the West End House, the Elizabeth Peabody House had a day camp during the summer months for children in the West End. Here children wait on Charles Street in the morning for their group leaders. (Courtesy of the West End Historical Association.)

Waiting outside the West End House in 1941 are Paul Wynn, Joe Szanowiz, Melvin Berger, Tommy Theodos, Anthony Schanafa, Butto Greenberg, Billy Landolfi, David Zanelli, and Joe Zanelli. (Courtesy of the West End Historical Association.)

A group of boys from the West End House eagerly jump on a truck that would take them to summer camp. A week in the country was a great change from life in the densely settled West End, and it was awaited annually with great excitement. (Courtesy of the West End Historical Association.)

Posing for their photograph on a diving board at summer camp are John Lo Blundo (standing), Joe Zanelli, and Pat Fiorello. These friends, all from Brighton Street, would experience a week in the country thanks to the West End House. (Courtesy of the West End Historical Association.)

Seven
WEST END LIFE

Joseph Lo Piccolo interviews Leonard Nimoy, aka Mr. Spock of Star Trek, at a reunion of former West Enders. Nimoy was born and raised in the West End and is a supporter of the efforts of those who chronicle and perpetuate the history and subculture of this neighborhood of Boston that was swept away by urban renewal. In the center is James Campano, editor of *The West Ender*. (Courtesy of the West End Historical Association.)

Scollay Square, named for 18th-century merchant John Scollay, was an active intersection at the turn of the century. The statue of Governor John Winthrop (1588–1649) on the right was sculpted by Horatio Greenough and was placed in the intersection, which was often referred to as Winthrop Square. The statue is today located in the Back Bay, in the garden of First and Second Church on Marlborough Street. (Courtesy of Frank Cheney.)

Looking up Cambridge Street, the underground tunnel for the streetcars running to Cambridge can be seen in the center of the photograph. Cambridge Street would be widened in the early 20th century, with the buildings in the center being demolished. The spire of the Old West Church can be seen on the left, the pinnacles of the Bowdoin Square Baptist Church in the center, and the tower of the Customs House, designed by Peabody and Stearns and built in 1915, on the right. (Courtesy of Frank Cheney.)

Cambridge Street, west of Staniford Street, was a charming part of the old West End. The Old West Church, used as a library at the time this photograph was taken, and the restored Otis House (on the left) gave this section of the street a Federal aspect. The stores on the right would eventually be swept away in the urban renewal of the late 1950s. (Courtesy of the West End Historical Association.)

Spring Street was laid out in 1733 and connected Leverett and Allen Streets. When this photograph was taken, it was a densely built-up neighborhood with apartment houses and tenements creating a solid block of housing. (Courtesy of the West End Historical Association.)

In this c. 1910 photograph, the activity of the West End streets is evident. On the left is Seiniger's Prescription Pharmacy. (Courtesy of the West End Historical Association.)

A woman walks toward Saint Joseph's Church at the corner of Blossom and McLean Streets about 1950. Notice the apartment houses that line the street on the right, all of which would be demolished for the luxury, high-rise apartment buildings of Charles River Park. (Courtesy of the West End Historical Association.)

Near the corner of Allen and Charles Streets, the wall of brick created an urban village that was densely settled. The use of red or yellow brick with limestone trim made for a distinctly urban feeling. (Courtesy of the West End Historical Association.)

Staniford Street ran from Cambridge to Causeway Street. The Mobil gas station on the right still exists, but the buildings on either side are long gone. The cupola of the Old West Church can be seen rising just above the building in the center. (Courtesy of David Rooney.)

Looking east on Cambridge Street, the cupola of the Old West Church peeks above the roofs of buildings that would eventually be demolished for a modern mall with ample parking spaces. Though most who lived in the West End—or live today on the western slope of Beacon Hill— rarely kept cars, this parking lot was a seeming necessity for a strip mall at the time of urban renewal. (Courtesy of the West End Historical Association.)

On the left of Cambridge Street is the site of the Holiday Inn—but, in the late 1950s, this area was a part of the neighborhood known as the West End. Stores, shops, and even gas stations lined the street, creating a pedestrian community for those who lived there. (Courtesy of the West End Historical Association.)

The West End Esso station was a Colonial Revival automobile station dating from the early 1920s. Seemingly "plunked down," this gas station with its arched windows and roof balustrade gave a distinctly Classical Revival feeling to the rear of these apartment buildings. (Courtesy of the West End Historical Association.)

A group of boys stops for a quick game of "penny ante" in front of a small grocery store in the West End. (Courtesy of the West End Historical Association.)

Photographed in 1941, Eaton Street was a charming cul-de-sac that was laid out in 1795 connecting Chambers and North Russell Streets. Though the West End is often referred to as a neighborhood of tenements and (unfairly) as a slum, the three-story bow-front house on the left emulated the style of housing being built on Beacon Hill and the South End at the same time. (Courtesy of the West End Historical Association.)

Mr. Ganek stands c. 1925 behind the counter of Ganek's Deli and Spa, which was at the corner of Phillips and Grove Streets. (Courtesy of the West End Historical Association.)

Ascending the stairs from the Blossom Restaurant, located at 103 Blossom Street, is a satisfied customer! The prices might seem ridiculous in this day and age; even in the teens of this century, the prices were quite reasonable for the hearty dishes served here. (Courtesy of the West End Historical Association.)

Three women converse on Spring Street in front of Broitman's Kosher Butcher Shop. The ethnic groups living in the West End at the turn of the century were so diverse that it could be a model for any city today. (Courtesy of the West End Historical Association.)

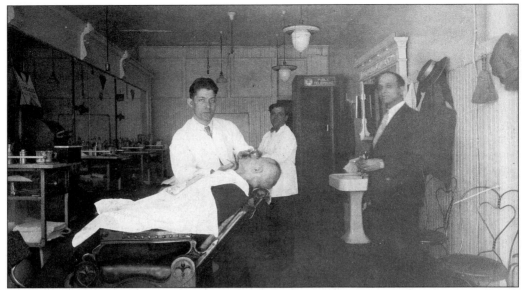

It's probably best to have someone watch as you are being shaved—especially if you are being shaved by a barber with a straight razor! The interior of this barber shop in the West End in the 1920s seemed quite luxurious, especially with the white-coated attendants. (Courtesy of the West End Historical Association.)

Jimmy Garrasi and his son Phil pose in their cobbler shop at 67 Staniford Street in 1941. It was a common occurrence to have worn-out soles of shoes replaced rather than discarding the shoes, as is often done today. (Courtesy of the West End Historical Association.)

The Morello family posed for their photograph in 1923. From left to right they are as follows: (front row) Salvatore Morello, Sebastino Morello, and Lena Morello; (back row) Joseph Morello, Gaetano Morello, Lucy Morello, Anna (Mignosa) Riera , and Maria (Riera) Morello. (Courtesy of Richard J. Morello.)

Posing on a pony in front of her home at 3 Ashland Street in the West End in 1940 is Rose (Vatalaro) De Salvo. Photographers would often visit neighborhoods in Boston with their cameras with an obliging pony to solicit business. (Courtesy of the West End Historical Association.)

Joseph and David Zanelli pose with their prized toy automobile in 1926 in front of their home on Minot Street. (Courtesy of the West End Historical Association.)

Liborio Lo Blundo puffs on a cigar as he leans against the entrance to his home at 75 Brighton Street. On the left is his neighbor, Joan Brewster. (Courtesy of the West End Historical Association.)

Al Tabashnick was a well-known character who seemed to fit right into the West End. Though an obvious street person, he often was asked to cantor at religious holidays in the neighborhood temples, appearing in flowing robes and singing in a deep voice. The next day, he would be walking the streets and picking trash. (Courtesy of Jules Aaron.)

"The Professor" was an intimate friend of Tabashnick. Sitting on the rear of an automobile in 1947 for his photograph, he is outside the Riverside Gardens at the corner of Auburn and Leverett Streets. (Courtesy of the West End Historical Association.)

Standing at the corner of Minot Street in 1937 are, from left to right, as follows: (front row) Rose (Vatalaro) De Salvo and Sal De Salvo; (back row): Ann (Russo) De Salvo, Tony Fati, Mike De Salvo, and Jane (Sciaraffa) De Salvo . (Courtesy of the West End Historical Association.)

Posing with their catch after a day of fishing at Salem Willows are, from left to right, Tony Puopolo, Willie, Pete, Sonny Puopolo, and ? Fama. (Courtesy of the West End Historical Association.)

Fran Mc Laughlin delivered ice and range oil in the West End—ice to keep food cool in an ice box (the predecessor of the refrigerator) and range oil for the stove to keep West End homes warm. (Courtesy of the West End Historical Association.)

Ice deliveries were a common occurrence 50 years ago. On the right is Willie Vicari, who had cut a block of ice the correct size to fit into an ice box. He holds a pair of ice tongs that allow him to carry the ice with ease. A block of ice, if one was lucky, might last two days, after which one placed a card printed with the word "ICE" in the window. (Courtesy of the West End Historical Association.)

Charlie Joyce and Mario Manzelli embrace one another in greeting in Mazur's Drug Store in the late 1940s. (Courtesy of the West End Historical Association.)

Mazur's Drug Store was a popular place in the 1940s. From left to right are Mary Fishera, Eleanor Capachiette, Frank Giannio, and Nina Bottari. (Courtesy of the West End Historical Association.)

Standing on Grove Street in 1938 are George Murphy, Mike Cataldo, and Frank Mafao. (Courtesy of the West End Historical Association.)

Standing outside Fox's Pharmacy at the corner of Grove and Phillips Streets in the early 1940s are, from the left, "Bunny" Leonard, Dick Oliver, Bert Perkins, and Fred "Tut" Johnson. (Courtesy of the West End Historical Association.)

A rubber-tire drive during WW II brought civilians and enlisted people to assist in the worthy cause. Gladys Shapiro, in uniform and second from the left, and fellow West Enders pass rubber tires to men standing behind the fence in front of the Joy Street police station in 1942. (Courtesy of the West End Historical Association.)

Posing in front of Recko's Meat and Grocery Shop at the corner of Brighton and Chambers Streets in 1943 are, from left to right, Teddy Lupo, Walter Kozol, Bill Piniak, and Roland Phillips. (Courtesy of the West End Historical Association.)

In 1943, "What's left of the gang (who were not serving in World War II)" posed for their photograph. From left to right are Paul Burroughs, Arthur Boss, John Burroughs, Nappy Hartnett, and Gabby Hartnett. (Courtesy of the West End Historical Association.)

Posing for a group portrait in Burke's Funeral Home on Chambers Street in 1946 are, from left to right, as follows: (front row) John Sullivan, Edward Fitzgerald, William Hunter, Charles Chivakos, Robert Downes, Joseph Kenny, and Warren Lufkin; (back row) John Bartholomew, John Beaujang, Robert Corrano, Daniel Leary, Robert Burke, Charles Emmons, and Frank McCoy. (Courtesy of the West End Historical Association.)

Posing in front of 25 Eaton Street in 1939 are Louis Berger, Clara Goldberg, and Max Berkman. (Courtesy of the West End Historical Association.)

Young patrons at the West End Branch of the Boston Public Library admire an exhibit commemorating National Book Week in November 1943. (Courtesy of the West End Historical Association.)

Peter Dembisky was a noted boxer in the West End in the 1950s. (Courtesy of the West End Historical Association.)

International Amateur Boxing Tournament
ITALY   GERMANY   UNITED STATES
UNDER THE AUSPICES OF

St. Joseph's T. A. Society, West End
BOSTON GARDEN
Monday Evening, February 3, 1930

The following classes will be contested : —

BOXING
International Classes — 135 lbs.,   147 lbs.,   160 lbs.
Heavyweight
Open Classes — 112 lbs.,   118 lbs.,   126 lbs.

Entries close Friday, January 31, 1930, with William H. Cuddy, 333 Washington Street, Boston.
Sanctioned by the New England Association of the Amateur Athletic Union.
A. A. U. rules to govern. The committee reserves the right to reject any entry.
All contestants must be registered. Register with J. Frank Facey, 36 Prospect Street, Cambridge, Mass.
Seats, $1.00, $1.50, $2.00, $3.00. 333 Washington Street, Boston, Mass. Room 314.
NOTE—Telephones, Liberty 8708—Hubbard 4642—Boston Garden, Capitol 3200.

Saint Joseph's Total Abstinence Society (a group that advocated no alcohol consumption) sponsored an amateur boxing tournament at the Boston Garden in 1930. These evenings were sponsored for enjoyment, without the inducement of alcohol to enjoy oneself. (Courtesy of the West End Historical Association.)

Members of the Saint Joseph's West End bowling team met at Daylight Alleys on Cambridge Street in the 1950s. Today, former residents of the West End still have a bowling league that meets on Wednesday evenings. (Courtesy of the West End Historical Association.)

Minstrel shows were once a popular form of entertainment, and here members of Saint Joseph's Church mug for the photographer. From left to right they are as follows: (front row) Sam Ponzo, Dick Russo, and Mario Manzelli; (back row) ? Bova, Leo Haley, and Ed Lyons. (Courtesy of the West End Historical Association.)

Mario D'Amato, a resident of the West End, sold newspapers throughout Boston in the 1950s. (Courtesy of the West End Historical Association.)

Bobby Block weighs fruit on a scale at Pat Rao's Market, which was at Charles Circle. (Courtesy of the West End Historical Association.)

Surrounding an unknown man in front of Mike's Variety Store at the corner of Ashland and Leverett Streets in 1940 are, from left to right, Sylvia Berger, Jane (Sciaraffa) De Salvo, and Grace (Coletti) De Salvo. (Courtesy of the West End Historical Association.)

Posing on the hood of a car outside Papa's Cafe on Leverett Street are Mary Carbel and ? Fitzpatrick. (Courtesy of the West End Historical Association.)

John Caljown stands in front of his friends; from left to right they are John Clifford, Bill Tobin, Tommy Adams, and Arthur De Gregorio. (Courtesy of the West End Historical Association.)

Posing in front of a car on Billerica Street are, from left to right, as follows: (front row) Frank "Blinky" Alessandro and Al "Muzzie" Cabone; (back row) Sal Pranieri, Teddy, and Ralph (the oil man) Contardo. (Courtesy of the West End Historical Association.)

The Charlesbank Apartments were built in 1907 on Charles Street opposite the Charlesbank. Edward Ginn, a civic leader of Boston and a well-known publisher, had a model tenement building constructed to ensure not only the comfort of the residents but to prove to builders that such a design could supercede the crowded, narrow tenements currently inhabited. (Courtesy of David Rooney.)

Posing in the Charles River Garden in 1953 are, from left to right, Butch Lo Piccolo, Victor Gjika, Richie, Philip Simileri, Joe Lo Piccolo, and Kermit Weinstein. On the right is the Elizabeth Peabody House on Charles Street. (Courtesy of the West End Historical Association.)

The narrow streets of the West End were never more hazardous than when a fire truck tried to hurry through them. A fire engine enters the intersection of Auburn and Chambers Streets, with one already parked in the middle of the street, to answer a fire alarm. (Courtesy of the West End Historical Association.)

The streets of the West End were the playground of the children. Here tricycles are in evidence with many youngsters enjoying an afternoon outdoors. (Courtesy of the West End Historical Association.)

These young girls jump rope outside their homes in the West End in the 1950s. (Courtesy of the West End Historical Association.)

Freddy Fishlin poses outside of the Pini family's home on Auburn Street in the 1950s. (Courtesy of the West End Historical Association.)

Smiling for the camera are, from left to right, Linda, Joyce, and Bill Crooks Jr. (Courtesy of the West End Historical Association.)

These three strapping young men on Ashland Street in the early 1950s are, from left to right, Tony Christopher (in his schoolboy parade uniform), Richard Settipane, and Sal Palmisano. (Courtesy of the West End Historical Association.)

Posing for their photograph in the dining room of their Phillips Street home are the following, from left to right: (front row) Julia Clark, Pavilla Jones, and U.S. Clark; (back row) Sisto Coletto, Florence Warren, Ria Jones, and Helen Clark. (Courtesy of the West End Historical Association.)

A bevy of West End beauties smiles for the camera on Christmas Eve in 1950. From left to right are Helen Johnson, Frances "Honey" Giardino, Marie Genovese, Connie De Stefano, Lorraine Mercurio, and Helen Limone. (Courtesy of the West End Historical Association.)

...mily ...ograph ...n the ...r ...et home ... From left ...Carol Lo ...andpa ...ncle Joe ...ncle Augie ..., and Peter Lo ...lo; the two boys in ...nt are Joe Lo Piccolo and Michael Lo Piccolo. (Courtesy of the West End Historical Association.)

The Vicari family poses for a photograph in their kitchen on Chambers Street. (Courtesy of the West End Historical Association.)

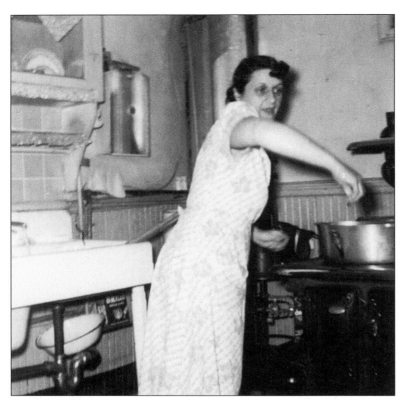

Elizabeth Christopher adds salt to a dish she is preparing in the kitchen of her Ashland Street home. (Courtesy of the West End Historical Association.)

After a good home-cooked meal, who could possibly resist a nap? Here, William Vicari dozes in his highchair in the kitchen of his parents' Chambers Street home. (Courtesy of the West End Historical Association.)

Eight
URBAN RENEWAL

Looking toward the West End in the early 1960s from the courthouse, much of the neighborhood had been swept away in what was termed "urban renewal." Cambridge Street in the foreground is still recognizable with the Old West Church and the Harrison Gray Otis House to its left, but old Saint Joseph's Church stands in stark contrast to a totally leveled neighborhood. (Courtesy of the West End Historical Association.)

A group of protesters stands in front of the Old West Church on Cambridge Street in the late 1950s to rally against the redevelopment of the West End by Jerome Rappaport. (Courtesy of the West End Historical Association.)

The Committee to Save the West End operated out of this storefront on Staniford Street. On the window were painted "The West End Minute Men" and "Don't Tread On Me," two slogans that bolstered the confidence of West Enders fighting the practice of urban renewal in their neighborhood. (Courtesy of the West End Historical Association.)

A woman stands forlornly in a parking lot in the West End as an enormous sign proclaims the brilliant future of the neighborhood—through urban renewal and the displacement of families. Financed through the Urban Renewal Administration, the City of Boston cleared the neighborhood of all people, houses, and almost every vestige of the former neighborhood. (Courtesy of the West End Historical Association.)

A commonplace scene in the late 1950s was that of automobiles being packed by residents of the West End who were evicted by the Boston Redevelopment Authority. Here, in a poignant image, a station wagon is packed to its gills and stands in front of the office of Modern Realty, until then a thriving real estate office. (Courtesy of the West End Historical Association.)

As residents moved from the West End, the vacant buildings were boarded up to preclude vandalism or arson. Here a group of children whose parents still have not relocated sits on the steps of a Greek Revival brick townhouse on Allen Street near Chambers Street. (Courtesy of the West End Historical Association.)

A well-known eviction of a resident of the West End who fought against leaving her home was referred to as the Elizabeth Blood Case. Mrs. Blood sits on the hood of her automobile as her possessions are removed from her home. The West End Project of the Boston Redevelopment Authority was a thorough, non-personal agency that effectively rid the neighborhood of all residents so that "urban renewal" could commence. (Courtesy of the West End Historical Association.)

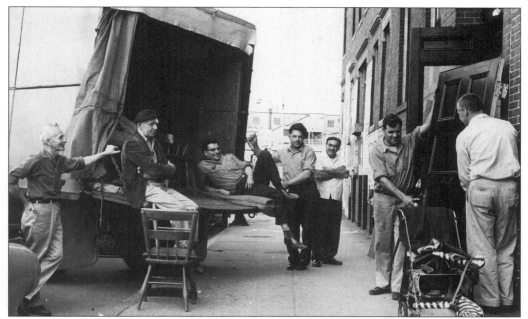

The movers who were packing Mrs. Blood's possessions take a break. This scene would be repeated many times over the next few months. (Courtesy of the West End Historical Association.)

John Mc Cormick, age 13, and Beth Eastman, age 4, were grandchildren of Mrs. Elizabeth Blood. Here they are taking a walk on a sidewalk that leads to utter desolation—a neighborhood that has been leveled on all sides of their grandmother's home. (Courtesy of the West End Historical Association.)

A crowd of spectators watches as the Old Howard is hosed down while the wrecking ball demolishes the stone facade. Once a pleasure palace with burlesque queens strutting their charms for the benefit of red-blooded Bostonians, the Howard saw its last breaths of life extinguished in just a few minutes, along with decades of memories. (Courtesy of the West End Historical Association.)

The demolition of Saint Mary's Church took little time. Here the remains of the wall behind the altar, with angels looking as if they are taking off in flight, is about to be grasped by the mechanical claw in the foreground. (Courtesy of the West End Historical Association.)

A doorway frames the interior of a building being demolished. A keystone with an expressive face cut in stone looks as if it is grimacing at the devastation surrounding it. (Courtesy of the West End Historical Association.)

A wrecking ball is suspended from this soaring arm that moves and swings at all in its path. A huge mountain of rubble and debris on the right represents homes that have already been swept away. (Courtesy of the West End Historical Association.)

Two dogs look out a window in July of 1964 at the demolition of the West End. On the left can be seen the Old West Church and on the right is the White Building of the Massachusetts General Hospital. (Courtesy of the West End Historical Association.)

Two residents of the West End gingerly pick their way through the devastation wrought by urban renewal. Though the image looks like the aftermath of WW II in a European city, it is a neighborhood of Boston undergoing a transformation—albeit a forced transformation! (Courtesy of the West End Historical Association.)

Looking up Staniford Street toward the Old West Church in the early 1960s, debris and piles of soil mark the former West End. The modern building in front of the rear wall of the Old West Church is the Schepens Eye Research Institute and the Boston Biomedical Institute. (Courtesy of the West End Historical Association.)

Looking like the King of the Hill, this young boy stands on rubble from demolished buildings in the West End. A modern, high-rise apartment building rises near Leverett Circle and the Science Museum on the right. (Courtesy of the West End Historical Association.)

By 1965, Bowdoin Square and Cambridge Street bore scant resemblance to the old West End. Granted, the Old West Church remained, but the modern, high-rise apartment buildings of Charles River Park rise from the cleared streets. On the right would be the site of Government Center with the JFK Building and Boston City Hall.

Rising high above the recently leveled West End were the Charles River Park Apartments. Sleek and modern, they could boast of views of the Charles River and were in close proximity to downtown Boston. On the right is the Science Museum on the Charles River. (Courtesy of the West End Historical Association.)

The West End

Oh how I wish I could go back again
To walk thru the streets that were once the West End
The city was poor, but the people were proud
And all were accepted as part of the crowd.
The Polish, the Jewish, Italians and Blacks
Were helpful and friendly, not planning attacks
The people were neighbors regardless of race
And life moved along at a very nice pace.
I think about Schnipper, a chubby old guy
Who sold us the fruit as he swatted a fly
Tabachnik would play his old violin
As he sat on the curb with it under his chin.
Lazzarro's had ice cream that tasted so great
A very nice place to relax with a date
On Fridays I'd dress in my favorite blouse
To go to a dance at the Peabody House.
The Winchell and Blackstone are where I was taught
They kept us in line and they taught us a lot
They knew education would give us the key
To open the doors of prosperity.
The West End was home, as my family agrees
My sisters were Dotty and Pat and Louise
And Antoinette, well she is my mom
My brother is Joey, my father was John.
A street we called "Barton" is where I resided
Without our agreement, our fate was decided
For urban renewal, they forced us to scatter
Our lives and our feelings, did not seem to matter.
That Rappaport fella did us all wrong
He sent us away from the place we belong
Our thoughts and our memories are all that remain
He broke all our hearts just for personal gain.
Frongillo, Kachoris, Ventresca and Smith
Are some of the people I hung around with
Where are the Butmans, Sidlowskis and Payzers
Dembickis and Hausers, Rausinos and Mazers.
On Testa and Mayo, I had a big crush
And Lynch and DeLuca, could cause me to blush
I think of the Charneys, the Rumas and Ross's
Strazzulas, Fitzpatricks, Kisalowskis and Kostkas.
So many good memories are still in my mind
I miss all the neighbors that I cannot find
But maybe one day we will all meet again
For all our hearts are in the West End.

—Josephine Martyniak Mulvihill

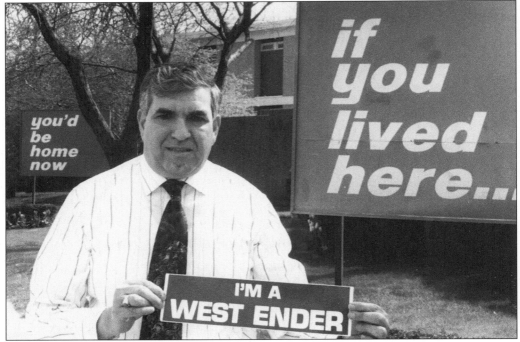

Joseph Lo Piccolo holds a sign reading "I'm A West Ender" in front of the well-known "If you lived here, you'd be home now" sign that was erected on Storrow Drive after the Longfellow and Whittier Apartments of Charles River Park were built in the mid-1960s. (Courtesy of the West End Historical Society.)

ACKNOWLEDGMENTS

I would like to thank the following for their assistance in researching this book on Boston's West End. In many instances, the following individuals have been of great support to my research and I greatly appreciate their continued friendship. The West End Historical Association, through the vitally interested Joseph Lo Piccolo and Richard Morello, loaned the majority of the photographs used in this photographic history and I very much appreciate their interest and support.

In addition, I would like to thank Jules Aaron, Paul and Helen Graham Buchanan, Reverend Gerald Bucke, James Campano (of *The West Ender*), Jamie Carter (my ever patient editor), Frank Cheney, Elise Ciregna, Lorna Condon (of the Society for the Preservation of New England Antiquities), Dexter, Edward W. Gordon, Sally Ann Kydd, James Z. Kyprianos, Joseph Lo Piccolo, the Massachusetts General Hospital, Richard J. Morello, the Old West Church, Raymond Papa, Reverend Michael Parise, William H. Pear, David Rooney, Anthony and Mary Mitchell Sammarco, Rosemary Sammarco, Sylvia Sandeen, Robert Bayard Severy, William Varrell, the Victorian Society, New England Chapter, the West End Historical Association and its supportive membership, and Rhoda Blacker and the staff of the West End Branch of the Boston Public Library.